The Velvet Glove

The Velvet Glove
My Journey into Diabolism

Actaea

COVENSTEAD PRESS
Buffalo, New York

Ave Magina Domina

Preface: Why this Book is Anonymous

There are a number of reasons to make a book anonymous, most of them dishonourable. This book is anonymous for the best of reasons, for what is included herein is an extant, living metaphysical system that uses the secret place of sin and shame that most of us have as a result of the Judeo-Christian upbringing we get in the English-speaking world. This is not the first time this system has been discussed, nor is it the first time it has been published by a brave and independent publisher. It is, however, the first time it has not been written about for massive public gain by a showy magician seeking to make a buck.

Since I am choosing to remain anonymous, I can write honestly about this system, and not worry about landing in court, sued by some frivolous American Biblebelt Republican for teaching his kids the power of naughty. I can also rest safely at night knowing that the schizophrenic freaks who might pick up this book and create lavish fantasies about me won't know where I live and who I am. Most importantly, I don't have to worry about breaking oaths I made under duress, an action that might otherwise cause me to worry about those who made me take those oaths hunting me down and doing me harm.

This last reason, more than any others, is why this book is anonymous. While paranoid fundamentalists create overblown fear about the path described herein by painting it as a highly organized, it is, in fact, an old fashioned, un-networked collection of groups which survive as remnants of a now-destroyed organized diabolist community from the late eighteenth century. The groups that exist now are independent shards of the great mirror of Diabolism, and this book exists to show the entire mirror, with the firm knowledge that these groups would rather destroy themselves than admit to being flawed, and would gladly destroy anyone who has seen their reflection in the whole mirror.

It is because this book is anonymous that I cannot convince you as to my expertise in this system. I cannot, safely, explain who am I and how I came to know these things. I cannot name names, I cannot give locations, and I cannot give my name. Rather than be burdened by this inability to demonstrate things with firm proof, I sincerely hope that the elegance and simplicity of the system herein described is proof enough as to the existence of the system, and that my little work is enough to allow those who would practice Diabolism to get the whole picture instead of the fragments they may have now.

That's not to say that this book must be read only by Diabolists. Indeed, if reading this book cures just one ignorant Pagan or Judeo-Christian of their view of the Left Hand Path as a lesser or weaker metaphysical system, or one that can be destroyed by praying hard and waving magic wands, then I have succeeded beyond my wildest dreams.

Chapter One: What is Diabolism?

Diabolism is a very misunderstood term. It is not Satanism, although Satanism can be a part of it. It is not Left Hand Path Magick, although that, too, can be a part of it. It is certainly not abusing others to get your will done, as the most idiotic of self-proclaimed Diabolists will try. Diabolism is a technique of tapping into the secret place of sin and shame created within each individual by the mores and standards of his culture.

It does not require Judeo-Christian culture, although modern forms of it are flavoured by Judeo-Christianity. What it does require is a dominant cultural paradigm that is restrictive and uses embarrassment and shame to enforce the cultural norms. Diabolism faded from the English-speaking world as psychology rose in power because they serve the same purpose—keeping people capable of surviving in their culture when their inner world is in conflict with it.

Freud called the parts of the mind that were the source for "unacceptable" drives the Id, and while modern psychology mostly disregards the idea of the Id, it still embraces "drives" as thoughts and unacceptable wants. These drives are seen as normal phenomena which have to be worked around. Diabolism is one such work-around.

A brief understanding of the mind in modern psychology is enlightening when discussing Diabolism. It has been intensely studied and well documented that when presented with a scenario our brain seems to list all possible reactions in flashes of thought. The brain, unburdened by morality as it is, lists ideas that our mind sees as morally unacceptable and this creates guilt inside of us.

For example, you might find yourself dealing with an obnoxious woman being unreasonable. Imagine, for example, that a teller is refusing to accept your identification for no reason whatsoever, or for trumped up reasons. Your brain lists hundreds of things you could do, from reasonable ideas, like going to another teller or another location, to unreasonable ideas, like screaming or threatening the woman, to absolutely ridiculous ideas, like climbing over the stile and ripping her heart out with your bare hands.

This listing behaviour is completely normal, and is based on the types of behaviours you have witnessed or experienced, including not only media violence and entertainment, but also the so-called "good" influences of church or school. If, for example, you learn about the Spanish Inquisition in the context of their wretchedness, hearing of their torture techniques as reasons for their evil, that information is still inside your head and somewhere, deep in your brain, you're wearing a red robe and giving that teller the *strappado*.

In cultures in which such thoughts are unacceptable, out of our control or not, we often feel guilt for having *thought* these thoughts. Freudian psychology excuses those thoughts by saying they come from the Id and therefore are normal, and modern psychology talks about influence and drives and excuses the thoughts by saying they are just random data, not actual desires. Neither form of Psychology, however, does much to deal with the guilt that is felt by the person for having these thoughts, except to say it is normal and that it is only is a problem when the guilt is in excess.

What, exactly defines "in excess?"
More accurately, **who** defines it?

In reality, only the actual individual feeling the guilt can define whether it is excessive guilt or not. Diabolists believe that *any* guilt for thinking, as opposed to *doing*, is wasted energy and pain. Since magi of any kind are trained to be aware of all (or most) of their mind's activities, magi feel this guilt and they must choose to either ignore the guilt (or the thoughts leading up to it) or they must learn to remove it by catharsis.

Diabolism is, at its heart, a catharsis on the ultimate level, in which the mage removes the guilt by confronting it in a way which does not disturb society (although it may disturb individual members of society) and is therefore able to move on without concern for the effects of the guilt on his will. At a larger level, Diabolism also provides a necessary balance to the forces of the universe.

In the Judeo-Christian world, the few successful campaigns against Diabolism have nearly always been followed by schisms which result in horrors being committed in the name of their religion. One thing that Diabolists of the past have claimed, and you can evaluate the veracity of it yourself, is that large, organized units of Judeo-Christianity intentionally set in place events that will lead to mass slaughter and pain, providing the catharsis the world needs in order to proceed forward.

I personally feel that the massive slaughter of innocents that has existed in Judeo-Christianity and its offshoot religions has been mainly the result of the religions being large. That notwithstanding, ancient Diabolist cults, existing before the creation of Christianity and in places where Judaism was only known of as a strange foreign tribal cult, did not have to put up with massive slaughtering by the major religions of their time, even when made illegal.

Diabolism is not an ancient cult in and of itself, it has changed and mutated based on whatever the dominant religion of the time and location is. It is, essentially, the cult of the *Adversary[1]*, he who opposes the way things are done. Diabolists may worship Pan in a culture in which maturity and sexual restraint are favoured, they may worship Bacchus in a culture in which altered states of consciousness are allowed only to the priestly elite. They may worship Kālī[2] as the dark mother

---

[1] Thus S-T-N, Satan, meaning adversary, is one being worshipped in some forms of Diabolism, but Satanism as practiced by many lacks the finesse required to be truly considered Diabolism.

[2] The Thuggee are an example of an Eastern Diabolist Cult, although they differ extremely from most Western Diabolists.

while surrounded by contemporary Hindus, or worship Satan in the midst of Christians. They may even worship a Goddess in the midst of a patriarchy, although none of these things are proof of being a Diabolist, just evidence thereof.

The term Diabolist comes from *diaballein*, literally he who throws across or who blocks your path, which itself comes from the Greek *diabolos*, which is often interpreted as slanderer but is perhaps best understood as he who calls you to account, rightly or wrongly. In the Hebrew and Greek Bibles, Satan, whose name means adversary, is also called *The Accuser*, and when he accuses in the Bible, he is not necessarily lying, but is, instead pointing out what people do not want to see.

Diabolists are essentially gadflies, irritating the hell out of the status-quo by questioning it, exploring it and stretching it. They provide the impetus for change in both positive and negative directions, gleefully pointing out what words really mean what people have really said and what they might really mean. They find the cracks in the armour of people's claims and they drive a wedge into those spaces requiring that the armour either be shucked or repaired.

Diabolism requires a high degree of personal integrity and intention, and probably more wisdom than most paths, and the path of Diabolism herein described is not for the weak of heart or the week of will. It is not necessarily for those of the dark side, although it is assuredly not a path of shameless self-sacrifice and shiny goodness. That which exists herein is the complete makings of a Diabolist life, from the beginning, with the tools for acquiring the rest.

Chapter Two: A Young Diabolist is Born

I began my initiation into Diabolism at ten, both because I was a bright young thing and because the Diabolist who initiated me was not. The grasping and half-hearted rituals of a would-be Satanist, overweight and balding at forty-five, were simple-minded, pathological child abuse, the domain of the moronic half-wit. He used his Satanism, or what he called Satanism, as justification for his mental ineptitude, and my mishandling at his hands nearly cost me the opportunity to truly pursue Diabolism as a lifestyle.

At sixteen, of age and angry at a world that denied me much, I was visiting the library of my local University, pursuing studies in the dark and occult arts, and happily finding that the dusty books inside the ancient and gothic library which described the Diabolism of one hundred years before. You must imagine me, for a second, to understand what a poor Diabolist I made...

Female, to begin with, and damaged goods at that, I did drugs and drank too much and wore my hair in a military surplus buzz cut. I affected an urban accent, and displayed weapons freely, although the authorities never fussed over me. I downplayed my intelligence, and skipped school more than I went, even though my grades were exceptional when I went. I had a problem with the world, and I made damn sure everyone knew it.

My studies had convinced me that I needed a mandrake root for the ritual I was planning, which would cause my abuser to die in a gory fashion absolutely unconnected to my physical actions. I did not need part of a mandrake root, but the whole thing, from under a tree where someone had been hanged, picked on the new moon, at exactly midnight, preferably in a churchyard.

I found such a churchyard by scouring the local history archives, conveniently sequestered in the same University building as the occult books. The churchyard had apparently been of some note in the nineteenth century for Diabolic activity, and the local legend was that the large (and famous) oak in the centre of the churchyard was used by a band of brigands to hang a local rector who'd been involved in some sort of naughtiness with a local dairymaid.

The churchyard was quite a bit out of the way, and the neighbourhood near it was fairly undesirable, so I did some early morning reconnaissance, bringing a mandrake cutting from my own garden to sink under the oak and harvest in a few months. When I got there, however, there was no need, for the warm ground beneath the tree was lousy with mandragora, which had flourished in the subtropical seaside town. It had just begun to flower, leaving the bushy leaves dotted with little violet flowers (my own mandrake had green flowers, but the plants were otherwise identical.) I planted my own piece of mandrake on the far side of the tree, away from the others, but made plans to come back on the new moon and harvest one of the ones already growing there, allowing me to complete the spell much earlier.

I won't go into the details of the spell, but I waited several days for the new moon and then, dressed in black from head to toe, hitched a ride to a club about three miles from the churchyard and walked through the dicey neighbourhood to the outer wall of the churchyard. Once I found a handhold in the stone, I was up and over, giving my eyes a chance to adjust to the blackness of the churchyard and listening carefully for any signs I'd been seen.

Once my eyes had adjusted, and I was certain I was alone, I crawled across the churchyard to the oak. The mandrake root I'd planted had sent up scraggly shoots, and the others were still in full flower. Clothed in black, I crawled prone across the soft dirt and leaves beneath the tree until I could just reach the first of the smaller mandrakes. I pulled out a small silver trowel and set to working the enormous root free of the soft ground.

After about twenty minutes, constantly stopping to see if I was being observed, I managed to extract the root, nearly one foot in length and of an exceptional shape. I placed it in a sack I'd procured for the occasion and slithered to the wall. As I turned back for one last evaluation of my surroundings, I was struck from the side by a shadowy figure with a glint in his right hand that I recognised as a knife.

This was not the jack knife or butterfly knife of the local thugs, but a triangular-bladed magician's knife, not dissimilar from the one that sat on my altar in my conjury back home. I tried to kick the knife out of the figure's hand, but he was easily twice as fast as me. Before I could even fully evaluate what had happened, I was incapacitated; a black gloved first flashing before my eyes before the darkness swallowed me.

I came to, lip bleeding, eye swollen, and with a huge slice of the mandragora in my mouth, which was tingly and slightly numb. I felt far less pain than I should have, and realized I must've swallowed some of it, and I immediately made myself throw up. Judging from the size of the chunks inside me, and the piece missing from the pilfered mandrake, which was beside me, I'd had far more than I needed to suffer poisoning, so I struggled to a pipe that stuck out of the ground in the churchyard and turned the tap. The water, no doubt provided for the plants, tasted foul and rusty, but I gulped it until I felt ready to burst then made myself throw up once more. Three more rounds and I felt clear headed enough to stand and try to collect myself.

Too weak to walk back to the club, I pulled myself to a shed in the churchyard, which was locked. An ancient bush of climbing roses grew up the side of it, however, and it had pulled away from the shed at the base. I slid between the bush and the shed, finding shelter a brief crawl away, hidden from the

churchyard path and any further attacks.
Then, dizzied from the mandrake, I lay down
and slept, not waking until the midday sun
shone through the leaves.

Afraid to move, I waited until nightfall
and crawled out. I was a wreck, but I still had
the mandrake, and a spell to do, so when I
made it home, and cleaned up, I performed
the ritual, pouring every ounce of my hatred
and rage into my actions. I fell asleep on the
stone floor of the conjury, and when I woke a
few hours later and stood up I felt as if I'd
just crawled out of my own grave.

The conjury was a stone shed on my
mother's property, used for this purpose since
before I'd taken up magic, as the flagstone
floor had long held chalk marks made by
people other than me, and the spaces between
the stones were full of colourful sand and the
remains of mysterious herbs. I'd taken to it as
a young child, and now as a teen it was my defacto apartment.

I struggled into the house, and washed
the sweat and dirt off of myself, managing to
make a semi-human visage out of my now
scabby lip and black eye via the heavy applica-
tion of cosmetics. The need for revenge now
burned brightly inside of me, although it was
no longer turned toward my former abuser,
who would be hit by a car and killed before
the year was out. I wanted the skin of the man
who'd had the audacity to punch me.

The same spell was out of the question,
as I lacked a focus, like the large lock of hair

I'd used for the vengeance spell or a sample of the man's blood. Instead, I would need to stake out the churchyard and get him when he came back for more mandragora. I knew from the way he'd tried to poison me that he felt I was trespassing on his crop, so I could assure myself that he'd return before the plants had started to bear fruit and the potency of the root declined.

I spent the next four weeks at the local gym, perfecting my fighting technique with the singular desire to give as hard as I'd gotten. I tried, and failed, to acquire a firearm, but I'd found a large iron-handled machete in a local junk store, and I was convinced that I was going to remove the hand of the guy who'd done this to me.

Every morning, I got up and went to the conjury, where I did push-ups within the circle I'd drawn, letting the sweat that was dripping off of my body feed the stones. I followed that with a trip to the gym, and then back to the conjury, where I would polish the blade of my machete with a cloth soaked in olive oil and my own blood. As I stroked the blade, I would repeat "May he that spilt my blood find his blood split with thee" over one hundred times.

Consulting all the books I could access, I limited my diet to bread, fruit, cream and honey and refused any drugs or intoxicants. I could feel the divine rage building within me, and as the days crept towards the new moon,

my singularity of purpose became clearer and
clearer.

I arrived at the churchyard the day of the
new moon, sneaking behind the gate as the
maintenance crew left for the day and taking
my place in the shelter of the rose bush. For
hours I sat alone, my mind focused only on
the desire for that guy to show up so I could
kill him, or at least put a serious hurt on him.

Shortly after midnight, I heard a car pull
up near the churchyard and a door shut. Soft
footsteps walked up the path and a figure
leapt the wall in the same place I had a month
earlier. I had no doubt, from the way he
moved, that this was my assailant from before. I shifted beneath the roses, and when he
was within a few feet I leapt out, the blade
flashing.

He shouted and two figures appeared on
our side of the churchyard wall. I swung the
blade at him, and kicked at him, but he was
simply too fast for me. Within a few moments, I was suspended between his two
thugs, and he was holding my blade, taunting
me. I could feel the rage bubbling inside me,
and the frustration, as he gloated about how
he was going to dismember me like some terrible Bond villain. Looking back, I see he was
just trying to panic me, but I was too angry
for panic.

Finally, the rage and humiliation were
too much for me to take, and I screamed
"die" as if I was drowning and his death was
my only life preserver. Although I hadn't

touched him, he fell back several feet, as if I'd
punched him in the chest and one of his thugs
dropped my arm and ran to him. He looked
me over with grudging respect and told the
thug to let his new student go.

Chapter Three: Apprentice

A Diabolist needs to be well trained in order to perform his art. While some Diabolists will learn from books or from people who learned from original Diabolist groups, the majority of the talented Diabolists become so by training with a real, live, human being.

Master Gregory[3] had trained with a teacher who had himself trained with one of the original Diabolist groups in London before World War I. As a rule, he did not take girl students, and he particularly frowned upon girl students who were "damaged," which he did not define as non-virginal, or as abused, but as lacking the will to define their lives outside of their abusers, or outside of anyone else, for that matter. When he took me in, I was still defining myself by what had happened to me as a child, and that meant my abuser still had power over me.

Diabolists play with power. While some Diabolists are submissive, the ability to control every aspect of your psyche is the primary goal of the first few years of training as a Diabolist, which is why it is so idiotic for Diabolists to try to train children, as my own abuser had. In order to give up one's will in a Diabolist rite, one must first know one's own will, and children, beyond a shadow of a doubt, do not know their own will. Indeed, many adults lack the knowledge of their will required to be a Diabolist.

[3] Not his real name.

My apprenticeship began with a frank assessment of my own fractured will. The reason that I was so very strong as a mage was because I had a singular focus on destroying the person who had harmed me. I hated him, and focused on the hate to the exclusion of all other things. At an intuitive level, I performed acts that increased my strength, despite not knowing why they did so, or even how.

When I woke in the morning at my house, the first thing I did once I was dressed and washed was walk into the area I had prepared as a conjury, the stone shed I was certain had held magic before. Once there, I would sit upon the floor in the centre of a very old chalk circle. My back straight, I would press the heels of my feet together in what I later learned was one of the power positions.

Energy flows through the body in circular patterns, much as the blood does. You can think of the energy that any mage uses as electricity that travels down from the centre of generation in the brain, and out through the extremities. If you are familiar with electricity, you know that some electricity in an energy field leaks out, especially where the field is forced to bend. By pressing the soles of the feet and the palms of the hands together, you conserve some of the energy you generate, causing it to slowly increase in circles around your body.

You can experience this by sitting with your back straight and the soles of your feet pressed together. Inhale slowly, pulling your feet and hands close to your body, then exhale, pushing the hands out and away from the body. Done properly, you will feel the energy moving in directed lines from your hands.

By doing this every morning in the conjury, I was increasing my personal energy so that I could direct the energy at any point in time that I had need of it. By moving the energy through my body, I was exercising the energy channels within my body, which would allow me to draw the energy at will. The majority of the exercises I did as an apprentice were designed to move the energy through the channels of the body in such a way as to accustom the body to the movement of energy through it.

You can think of it as drawing channels through the sand with running water. Each time you draw the same channel, you compact the sand around it, and make it firmer and stronger. When you pass energy through your body, it gets easier and easier until you can control it with nothing more than a thought.

For over a year, my only exercise as an apprentice was to rise in the morning and meditate for an hour, then try to get my life in order in such a way that I could devote myself fully to study. During this time, the man who I had wanted dead died unexpectedly (well, unexpectedly to him!) and this helped, but my teacher was correct in realizing that his death was not enough to make me capable of functioning at any level appropriate for heavy-duty magic.

I would leave the conjury and go to a local art school, where I studied drawing on and off over time. Master Gregory told me that art was worth studying for magic, because the ability to deconstruct the world into lines and shades of gray was a valuable skill, and since I had a free ride to the exclusive school, I set to it with a dedication I'd never had before. My teachers and mentors assumed I had gotten wise to the need to get an education, but the reality was that doing well in these classes was part of my training.

Between classes, I would find a position above the other students, in a tree, on a slope, at a second story window or elsewhere, and set to both draw and watch them. My goal was to learn which of the students had innate magical talent and who did not. After a few months of this, I had identified a dozen students with some degree of power, and I found a way to get into each of their lives.

An untrained magical talent is a danger not just to himself, but also to others. A common phenomena caused by a strong talent and a lack of training is known as the poltergeist or noisy ghost. It is seen most often in teens around the time of puberty, and while parapsychologists tend to view it as the result of trauma, it has been my experience that most poltergeist activity is the result of an untrained magical talent facing the normal stresses of everyday life.

A trained mage of any kind is capable of tapping and storing the power of an untrained magical talent. Since those who use energy are the ones most directly affected by the flow of energy, it behoves us to disarm the ticking time bombs of untrained talents before they create effects that disturb our carefully laid plans.

The easiest way to siphon energy off an untrained talent is through slow, consensual physical contact. Sexual contact is usually too exciting to serve as a functional method, but a slow backrub will work for most people. Simply run your hands one way to draw the energy into your hands and the other way to move the energy from your hands into your body. Trained mages also use a variation on this technique to exchange energy between each other.

Between building my own energy and siphoning it off of my tortured artists, I was able to engage in major workings without the need for exhausting myself. Magical energy comes from the easiest available source when you are doing a working. The first layer of energy expended is that which is created at the moment of the ritual, the next layer comes from your internal metaphysical stores, and the layers that follow come from your physical energy and the energy of the land or artefacts around you.

It is easier to draw from yourself than to draw from the land or artefacts around you, and many poorly trained mages, or those who find drawing from the land and local artefacts objectionable for some reason, will actually make themselves ill by using their physical energy for their magic. Reports of heart attacks, stroke and hypothermia during large workings have existed in the metaphysical community for years. I have both witnessed and experienced this final problem, as a working that just needs the slightest extra push is a perfect time to convert heat energy to magical energy, even if it is not terribly efficient.

Master Gregory joked that every portrait of a mage that has passed down to us through time is in front of a roaring fire, and half the time the mage is covered with a blanket, and if you've ever topped off a spell with your body heat, you'll understand why.

In addition to gaining my power and focus, I was required to participate in a minor working at least once a week and a major working once a month. Most of these involved strengthening the shields on my own conjury and that of Master Gregory. Most buildings naturally create shields because the flow of energy, whether seen as magic or even wind, is forced around a building.

Mages believe that energy naturally flows around the world. The way this energy is rationalized varies. Some people see it as connecting through a vast series of ley lines. Others see it as a massive sheet that moves across the land with the winds. I don't know how it works, but I know that it is there. I see it when I close my eyes and feel it when I move through it, and buildings cause it to bend and flow, just as if water was pouring around them.

That being said, the natural form of buildings (and standing stones, groves of trees, lakes, mountains, etc.) cause a natural shield that even the least talented mage can augment. The simplest way to do this is just by taking the energy you have built up and pushing it onto the natural barrier. Visualisation is the technique most start with, but as you visualise, you quickly discover physical sensations that are powerful guides to doing it right.

In the first year of my training, I went from constructing vague domes of light that began and ended at the barriers of physical structures to thin, potent coatings of light that glowed with an eldritch flame to the naked but trained eye. My master was very proud of my ability to shield things, and to move energy from one place to another, and I would later come to discover that all mages, Diabolists or otherwise, can be divided into four main talents, of which this energy sculpting talent was one.

The most common talents are called (often derogatorily) batteries and they are mages who don't have any real talent for manipulating or even tapping the power that they have. They make up about half of the mages in the world. Very strong batteries are sometimes called "psychic vampires" because untrained talents will feel drained and tired after being in close proximity to them. Batteries naturally draw energy into themselves and store it. They tend to use the power in sudden, sharp bursts, often with interesting effects.

A battery, for example, might break glass or cause lights to malfunction if they experience strong emotions, or they might miss an auto accident by inches, only to have the airbag deploy despite no damage to the car. A strong battery talent often interferes with magnets, so computers, battery cells, flash drives and magnetic discs might be at risk near these people.

Less common, but still making up about one-third of all talents is the Natural Null. A Natural Null has no natural magical energy, and is generally not aware of magic going on around them unless trained. What makes them different from the magically blind (the majority of people in the world) is that they are capable of focusing and directing the energies of others.

While it might seem like this would make one a bad mage, there is a lot of evidence to suggest that most of the really excellent mages in all of history have been Natural Nulls, because in order to be proficient as a Null, a person must be meticulous in their studies and perfect in their rituals. A battery can usually work around problems by just expending more power, but a Null must have all the lines in the right place in order for anything to work, and when it works, it is generally more elegant and potent than anything the rest of us do.

While it is a common talent, it is not common for Nulls to excel, but when they do they are the greatest of mages, because they are not swayed by the sensations and emotions that affect the rest of us. At least one great Diabolist, whom I shall not name for fear of offending his followers, was, to quote a student who learned at his feet, the Null of Nulls.

I had the opportunity to meet this student of the Null of Nulls, my Master's Master, an elderly man who was a part of this great Diabolist's inner circle, a man who, even old and infirm, made me jump when he ran his hand down my arm in a complex sigil, I could feel the energies inside me fall into rigid little lines, like soldiers lining up for a general.

His sigil worked like the third of the talents, the Sculpere, or Energy Sculptors, who are also called Catalysts. Sculpere have a natural ability to make energy more efficient, which allows it to be better directed and moved. I was identified as a Sculpere early in my training, as many young mages are. To the inner sight, a well trained Sculpere causes the natural energy fields around them to bend and flex to better fit into their places. It is, in many ways, the most useful of talents, but I am biased.

The fourth, and rarest kind of talent, is that of the Therion[4], or Wild Talent (from the Latin for wild animal.) Since it is so rare, many think it is the most powerful, but it is not. It is merely the most chaotic. The term has been used to refer to people who exhibit all, or many, of the characteristics of the other three talents, or whose talents surpass all others, but it is most accurately described as people whose talent, despite all efforts to contain it, waxes and wanes over time or otherwise acts like an untrained beast.

In a Diabolist cabal most Therions are shunned, which is a shame, because they often have great powers when their powers work and occasionally they can be trained to tap into their powers in more predictable ways. Unpredictability in magic is never a good thing.

[4] When Crowley used the term, he was referring to himself as *The* Therion, The Beast, of the Book of Revelations, while simultaneously thumbing his nose at non-Thelemite Diabolist groups.

Chapter Four: Ritual of the Second Year

My first year in the cabal was actually fifteen months, as the cabal counts time from one birthday to another, and I was a few months before my birthday on that night in the churchyard, so it was the night of my eighteenth birthday that I became a full member of the cabal, although I would still be an apprentice to Master Gregory for a while.

My first task that day was to clean and shield the cabal's shared conjury. Master Gregory's house featured a large conservatory that was built in the 1960s for this purpose. From outside, it looks like a typical Victorian greenhouse dome, with frosted glass panels and a centre vent. Within, it is approximately twenty-five feet in diameter, with a series of doors and nooks behind black satin curtains. A large iron and glass electric chandelier hangs from the centre, where two large beams intersect. The glass itself is said to be leaded, and therefore better shielded, but it seems normal glass to me.

The floor is packed earth with a layer of sand, and the sun streaming in the windows during the day makes it warm past midnight. Cleaning the conjury consisted of taking down the curtains (all twenty) and washing, drying and pressing them (only five would fit in the washer at a time, so this, itself, was a difficult chore) scrubbing the wood panels behind them with wood soap, cleaning all the regalia in cabinets I had access to (there were three cabinets and a cupboard forbidden to my rank) washing robes, polishing candle cups and the altar, washing the windows and lights and finally sweeping and refilling the sand.

In addition, as I cleaned the wood, I pushed as much of my energy as I could stand into the shields of the conjury.

All told, it took me about six hours, after which I felt physically and magically drained. My master had a spa, and I went to soak myself, and eventually fell asleep inside the water, not waking until one of the initiates came to fetch me. Taking a bath is an underrated magical act. The natural properties of water remove not only the dirt and debris of the physical world but also the metaphysical and energetic debris of the rest of the world.

Limp, and as weak as a newborn foal, I allowed the initiates to dress me in a simple white open robe, a sign of my status as new to the world and the group. Most people see the colours white and black as indicating beginning and expert mages, but in Diabolism, the masters of masters tend to wear greys and greens, which are colours that indicate liminality. The principle of liminality is vital to understand in magical practice.

Essentially, liminality means "doorwayness" or "sitting on the threshold" and refers to those things that mark the spaces between and are neither a part of nor separate from the places they separate. For example, imagine that you are standing in the exact doorway of the front of your housing. You are not indoors, although you can reach indoors. You are not outdoors, although you can reach outdoors. You are only accurately described as being in the doorway, or as being simultaneously both indoors and out and neither indoors nor out.

The liminal world is the world of the mage. He draws lines and uses power to be there and not there. He uses magic, and as a result is both a part of normal human culture and not a part of it. He is also part of the magical culture (the culture of ley lines and gods and energy) and simultaneously not a part of it.

To demonstrate this, my own master wore a robe of steel velvet, black cloth flocked with silver, which rippled and shifted colours as he moved. In the time I slept, a large wooden altar was set up in the conjury. A very large collection of mages was on hand, several of whom I had never met in this capacity. The altar itself glowed with energy. I was so drained that the energy seemed to draw me there, and I lay down upon it without needing to be told to.

My robe was open and I was exposed to the night sky and the score of mages in the conjury, but I did not feel even a second of shame, not because I was comfortable with my body, because I was not (and am not) but because I was so drained and so tired that it all felt like a dream.

One by one the mages of the cabal came up to me and drew delicate runes upon my skin with sable hair brushes. From my toes to my face, each of them drew complicated spells, which bound me to the group and the group to me in hundreds of different ways. The runes burned with hot and cold like eucalyptus or cayenne oil, but the inks were mostly scentless, just a vague odour of heme like old blood or rusting filings.

The air around me began to fill with mist and steam. I worried for a moment, then realized the ink was likely filled with mandragora or a similar substance and that this rite would take place in the space between consciousness and unconsciousness — a liminal world. Master Gregory loomed above me, his robe now making him seem to be made of flowing metal. Many of his words were lost to me, but several times he and the voices in the mist asked me questions which I answered truthfully, the words pouring from my mouth even as my brain formed the answers.

I was quizzed on my knowledge, asked about my sexual history, forced to promise to not expose the cabal members or our secrets, asked to pledge fealty to my master and his masters and much more. As I pledged these things the ink upon my body grew hotter and hotter until I felt as if the flesh on my body was being seared away, but I could not scream. Everything that came out of my mouth was calm, as if there was another being inside of me saying the words.

I stood up, now fully within the other world, and walked to a pedestal of flame. Upon the pedestal was a black book, and I traced my name upon the open page of the book, seeing it spring there in flames of its own. When I was signed, I turned around, and Master Gregory was there, his hand out. He led me back, upon a path that wound through a land of mist and flame, and led me to a place beside an altar that was a duplicate of the one in the conjury.

I spoke the oath of apprenticeship, agreeing to serve my master in all things and in all ways until I was his equal in power or better. Tears rolled down my face as I felt powerful relief and relaxation pour over me. He would be responsible for my food and lodging, my safety and my health. Literally, all I would need to worry about was serving him until I outranked him or my name was called out from The Black Book and I was to serve another elsewhere.

Deep inside of me, I felt this core of shame and anger. I was nude, in front of strangers, doing things my parents, even as progressive as they were, would find offensive to their God. I felt my body flush, and as I stood and then lay upon the altar my entire body chilled with doubt and fear. I felt it flow over me like a cold wave, and the fear and shame made me even more fearful and angry.

I was a mage! I wasn't even a Christian! I was a modern, liberated woman and here I was blushing like some Victorian chamber-maid who'd walked in on the master and his wife. The more I felt the shame, the deeper my anger at myself and my fear that I was not what I claimed to be. The more I feared, the colder I got, until it seemed like the cold was as intense as the flame had been.

I felt my body lifted, and saw a blade held over my heart. I closed my eyes and prepared to die, convinced the master and the others had found my secrets, seen my shame and now were going to discard me, since I knew far too much. The blade traced a thin line from my collarbone to my navel, and it felt like the cold was ripping out of me, pouring through the hole as my skin split open.

Strong hands ran down me, flame again, burning away the cold. I felt the heat building inside me, deep inside my womb, and I began to labour and work to move it from me as if in childbirth.

My body ceased to respond to my commands. All at once I could see though twenty-one pairs of eyes, feel twenty-one sets of thoughts, smell through twenty-one noses and taste with twenty-one mouths. I was made love to and made love to myself, I watched and experienced. I was everywhere and everything and eventually launched up, far above the conjury, propelled high until the earth seemed like a small bead of green in a field of bright stars.

I was one with the cabal, and one with the universe, and power exploded from between my legs with a feeling both orgasmic and torturous. I heard my screams, and then listened to the sound of a distant voice sobbing and begging, and realized the voice was my own.

My master spoke to me, words that even now in my mind I can feel the meaning of but not know exactly. I answered him, and it was as if a lifeline were tossed to me, bringing me back to reality.

I opened my eyes to face his, and heard and felt as he told me to sleep. I passed out then, and was aware at the periphery of a ritual going on above me, my body and blood the eucharist of the rite, shared amongst the cabal even as I shared with them. My flesh was the altar, my energy the power, but there was no more me, there was only the cabal, and my energy was theirs.

For the first time in my life, I belonged.

Chapter Five: Apprentice

When I woke the next morning, my skin was pink and raw as if I had been scrubbed with a floor brush. I felt hung-over, and exhausted, and I had a dull ache between my legs. A woman I did not know before the prior evening came in and smiled at me very gently.

"You did *very* well last night," she told me in a soft voice.

I didn't know what to say, so I shrugged, and she smiled again. "Master Gregory always pushes his students to their limit during the initiation rite, and he said that your limits were higher and stronger than any he could remember."

"Thank you," I blushed.

"It was not a compliment," she told me. "I have never seen much energy pass within those walls. You are truly a good addition to our cabal, even if you are altogether too young."

I sat up, but I was so dizzy that I laid my head back down quickly. She patted me on the head condescendingly. "There, there, girl, rest." She handed me a cup of tea and propped me up on a pillow, taking a seat beside me.

I stared at her, waiting for the explanation or monologue or whatever it was that brought her here, but she just sipped at a cup of tea and read a novel on her lap. I laid my head back down and closed my eyes, and at some point, the cup was removed from my hand.

I felt like I'd run some sort of marathon, my body being simultaneously pleasantly exhausted and sore. It wasn't long before I passed out again, and a different woman was in the room the next time I awoke. I tried to get out of bed to relieve myself, and it felt as if my legs were made out of sponge. The woman, another member of the cabal I knew only by sight, helped me walk across the room and later back into the bed.

I slept for a total of three days, with a couple of brief breaks. Four of the cabal's six female members took turns tending to me, and I later found out they had all volunteered. Master Gregory, knowing I had used mandragora in a number of spells before the initiation rite had used an ink with nearly three times the mandragora he would've usually used. As a result, I had taken the necessary journey to near death's door, but in doing so had put my body through far more than most others did.

Most people think the sexual aspects of Diabolism are the result of some sort of perversion that Diabolists have and which is expressed in their rites. In other words, in order to be attracted to Diabolism, most people must be attracted to fetish, or BDSM, or other paraphiliae.[5] In my experience, however,

---

[5] Paraphiliae, or paraphilias, are so-called nonstandard sexual interests or pleasures, and for the most part are non-criminal in nature and commonplace.

these paraphiliae are a direct result of the Diabolist's place as a shaper of the energies which are generated by puritanical and Marionist cultures trying to exert social control upon the world by restricting the natural energies of mankind.

If tomorrow, we all woke up and no large groups were attempting to enforce control over personal sexuality, and we were simultaneously able to break the training these groups indoctrinate us with, we would find that the powers used in Diabolism simply withered away. They exist because the deep consciousness shared by humankind, constantly fed a diet of what is wrong and not allowed by self-appointed overlords, craves that which is forbidden. Left on his own, without this indoctrination, humankind can regulate itself. The true vicious criminal, the child rapist, the murderer, cannot get away with his crimes in an open society, because when we are not afraid to do things for ourselves, we cull such things from the herd with impunity. Furthermore, without the need for privacy that the secret place of sin and shame within us all requires, there is no one who can hide his actions, and no one who would want to.

In the Bible, we are told that Adam and Eve were not ashamed of their nakedness until God made it so. This is an accurate metaphor for the effect of puritanical and Marionist control over society. That is not to say that society was free before Christianity.

Christianity is merely the "new boss" as it were, and it enjoys social control at a time when the social controls of the past (primarily control over ownership and reproductive rights of women) are ineffective because of science.

As long as one group is capable of completely dominating another, the controls they exert create desires in humankind. If you teach that women must be powerless, or that they are the root of all evil, making women the centre of a ritual, the root of power, and making their body the shared eucharist of a community reaches into the false forbidden— the things not allowed in order to exert social control—and when it touches that false forbidden, it explodes with power.

This is why Diabolism exists. Diabolism is a direct result of a majority dictating that things that are not an insult to our existence be stopped for no real reason. Those who stand against these meaningless laws are servants of The Adversary. The Adversary is Satan to the Christians, Bacchus, Pan and the Faeries to our ancestors. It is not an entity, although these may be entities, but a state mankind has created–the secret place of sin and shame.

As I recovered, this was explained to me once again. I tingled with the excitement of serving The Adversary, and as soon as I was able, I went to the large bedroom that served as Master Gregory's office and begged to be shown more. My entire body shook with lust

—not lust for Master Gregory, or any of the things he or the cabal did with me—but with a burning need to serve anything that opposed the same status quo that had injured me as a child and is still causing harm to millions today. Any energy I could raise that would fight the so-called spiritual warriors that seek to control the world by any means, ethical or otherwise, was energy I wanted to raise.

I begged Mastery Gregory. Standing there, in a nightgown, my skin still pink from the initiation rite, my legs still weak, my lips dry and cracked and my voice hoarse, I eventually dropped to my knees and just wept. Here was my chance to see that no one suffered as I had every again. I felt like I had the ability to take on the whole other side and win.

Master Gregory stood and struck me across the face, not as hard as he had in the churchyard, but hard enough to make my entire body twitch. He forced me to recite, once again, the oath of apprenticeship, and when I got to the line about serving my master in all things, he stopped me.

"Who do you serve?"

"You."

"And who do I serve?"

"The Adversary," I answered.

"Exactly." He pulled my face up to look into his eyes. "I serve Him, and you serve me. When you are my equal, or better, then you will serve him as you see fit. Until then, I will call on you as needed."

What I thought at the time was cruelty was actually brought about by deep love. Like most of the newly initiated, I was punch drunk with the power that had gone through me, and if he'd told me The Adversary wanted me to jump into the sea and drown, at that moment I would've done it gladly.

For the next two weeks, I would live, sleep and eat within fifteen feet of my master or his wife, a glorious woman whom I will call Jessica. It was this woman who tended me when I first woke from the ritual, and she would comfort me in the night when the inevitable nightmares came.

For reasons we don't understand, undertaking the mysteries of The Adversary taps into something deep inside that is definitely disturbed. For the first few days nightmares that haven't haunted you since you were a child will creep into your head and disturb your sleep the way they did when you were young. If, like me, you had real living nightmares of abuse or neglect, the nightmares verge on the edge of flashback and can last weeks.

When the nightmares came, Jessica would wake me, by stroking her hands across my face. I would dream, then, of cool water washing me, or the gentle lapping of a cat on my eyelids or nose. I would relax first, and then wake, and she would ask me where I was and what I was dreaming.

Jessica was a battery, and when I was having the nightmares, a time when others might experience poltergeist or other disruption, she sat there siphoning the power off of me, literally the sensation of cool water when I felt like I was walking in the desert.

Slowly the shimmer around Gregory started to fade, and I began to find myself more and more attracted to Jessica. When she touched me, it was like all the wounds inside of me and out healed, like she reached deep into my soul and smoothed out the rough edges. Two weeks after my initiation, I moved to a small bedroom, more of a monk's cell than a true room, just outside their bedroom door.

I found it nearly impossible to sleep without the rhythm of their breath beside me, and when I finally fell asleep it was fitful and disturbed with visions of rape and pain. Eventually, I woke to Jessica beside me, her lips pressed against mine, her breath slowly drawing energy out of me.

I wrapped my arms around her neck; a drowning victim pulled to the surface, and let her pull me to a stand and into the bed with her and her husband. Gregory seemed displeased at first that I was returning to the room, but as Jessica worked me out of the sweat suit I was sleeping in, covering my back and neck with kisses, she seemed to send him a message without speaking, and he quickly began to help her.

In moments, I was being made love to, not merely screwed, but lovingly and gently touched, caressed and entered. I was exhausted before they began their ministrations, and I soon found myself floating in the world of liminality once more, between consciousness and unconsciousness and then pleasure and pain.

Master Gregory grabbed me, hard, at the base of my neck and my body stiffened, like a kitten lifted by its mother. My nipples jumped erect, and I clenched, trembling with excitement. Jessica made a sound, deep within her throat that was simultaneously stimulating and terrifying and brought ropes from somewhere[6] to bind me to the bed.

For what seemed the whole of the night they tormented me with pleasure, using a host of sensations to test my limits. Several times I began to flash back to my childhood and the terror I felt at the hands of the idiot who had molested me, and Jessica sensed it every time it began and started to whisper in my ear, telling me the date, the time and where and who I was. They kept me talking the entire time they worked on me, interspersing the times of pleasure and lovemaking with mild torture, candle wax, pinching and light slapping. Once, when the flashback came especially hard, Gregory slapped me in that backhanded way he always punished disobedience with and made me stare into his eyes as he fucked me, asking me a number of the questions he had asked during the initiation, keeping me in the moment, not allowing me for a second to

---

[6] I was later to find these were stored in a box under their bed.

leave the time-space he was manifesting inside of me.

I have no idea how long they spent on me, and I was not allowed to finally dissolve into an impossibly long and intense orgasm until the sun had already risen. Though I would've preferred to say that at that time I then turned and made love to them, I passed out before I'd caught my breath, and woke up hours later in a pile of flesh and rope and various toys and torture items.

The sound of my breathing changing was enough to wake the others, and Jessica wrapped her legs and arms around me possessively and informed her husband that they were keeping me.

She was enough of a battery to store every ounce of the energy her husband and I gave off as the amorous exertions increased in number and intensity. She also was the most powerful empath and sensopath that I would ever meet in the whole of my country's Diabolist community and could achieve orgasm merely by standing within fifty feet of a man or woman who was experiencing it, even without visual or auditory contact. If she knew the person well, she could share their experiences from across town if she had a focus, such as a picture or a piece of their hair, and we never tested the functional limits of her ability.

This power actually made Gregory a better Master, because he would use signals from her in ritual to know exactly when a person

used as a focus in a ritual had entered the
space-time of liminality required to make a
ritual particularly effective.

Soon after I rose, Master Gregory
washed and left for his mundane job and Jessica went off to the garden to go about the
tending of her roses and apples. A well trained
eye would notice the enclosed yard and conservatory boxes were also full of Indian
Poppy, Salvia Divinorum and three varieties
of mandrake, but to most of the neighbourhood she seemed little more than a proper
little wife, tending the plants and kissing her
husband a tender goodbye at the front before
he got into his distinguished car and drove
off.

They had a maid, herself a Diabolist, but
not a member of our cabal, so she was not
permitted in the Master's room or a number
of other such places in the house, including
the conjury. This left the rest of the chores to
the lowest level of the cabal, and that meant
me.

The system of the house was elegant. All
doors had period medallions, circles in the
wood carved to look like round bunting, and
at the centre of each of the three medallions
on each door was a piece of semi-precious
stone. Mother of pearl meant the room was to
be considered public. Onyx or jet meant the
room was restricted to cabal members, and
thus not tended by the maid. Snowflake Ob-
sidian meant it was limited to those of the first
order within the cabal, which I, an apprentice,

was not part of, and hematite meant it was restricted to the highest of orders. If a door were locked, it was to be considered restricted and if it was both unlocked and not closed, it was to be considered public.

There were no locks on the majority of doors, but the enchantments on the restricted doors were such that one could feel them before one could see them, and that was enough to banish curiosity.

I was still an apprentice, and of the lowest order, and now I felt indebted further to my master and his wife. So I put on my least fashionable jeans and shirt, bound my hair up and headed to the kitchen, to immerse myself in vacuums and dusters, sponges for scrubbing walls and the lemony scent of woodsoap.

A number of rooms had old wood floors that could only be scrubbed by hand, and as my hands went in circles with the floor brushes, I would find my mind entirely blanking out, for long periods of time. The harder I worked, the less I thought, and the less I thought the more focused I seemed in the evening, when the master came home and the mistress returned from her shopping and various charity efforts.

When her lady's circle, terribly old fashioned and appropriate women, came to the house to have a meeting, I was introduced as her new maid, what she called an "upstairs maid," which apparently meant I was not well trained in serving tea and sandwiches to old biddies.

As the days turned to weeks, I began to think of myself not as a person but as a part of the house. My days consisted of cleaning, of polishing glassware and silver that always seemed to shine less than they needed to. My nights consisted of serving the needs of my master and mistress. They took to calling me "girl" and occasionally by the secret name I'd gained within the cabal.

Slowly, I think I began to go mad.

Chapter Six: Less than human

By my fifth month as an apprentice, I had cut off all contact with my family, completed my studies at school and withdrawn, ceased to answer the phone, surf the net or watch television. Even music and the company of other Diabolists began to be things I lost interest in. I had begun the silent dissent out of personhood that is part of a true mage's training.

At first, I felt ignored, only welcomed to the table or the bed when I had something to contribute, then later only when the whim struck my betters. The maid was my only contact with the outside world, and she spoke little to me.

At the time, I thought this was the experience of all beginners to a cabal, but I was later to discover that, unlike the metaphysical groups I had read about in the past, cabals decide the eventual placement of students when they accept them. They find a student whose true calling is to lead and make them leaders, they find a student whose true calling is to dabble and train them to do so. My master and mistress were training me to be as they were, leaders and teachers, and leaders and teachers required stronger techniques than other apprentices received.

The cabal, including the first rank members who were not allowed to attend my initiation and myself, numbered thirty people in total, but my master served as a hub and central contact for Diabolists and those of al-

ternate communities from across Britain. Satanists, some with slave girls who acted like
footstools for their masters, fetishists with
servants in bondage and ceremonial magicians
with brooding natures all passed through the
doors to bring information or techniques to
my master, and I was allowed contact with
none of them, sitting at the top of the stairs
where I could just barely see them and not be
seen myself.

For a few instances, I was locked in my
tiny cell across from the master's room for a
party, forbidden to make even a noise, and
once I was tied up, my ears and eyes covered,
my hands and legs bound up with rolls of
gauze like a mummy. I hallucinated, in that in-
stance, without the need for any of the drugs
or other techniques. I floated up, and out of
the basement where I was bound and into the
conjury, where I knew my master was and I
was forbidden. Inside, my master had another
young mage serving as his altar.

He furiously buggered him and beat him
with a small scourge tipped in metal, which
drew thin lines of blood from his back. I saw
his hands and legs were bound to an altar, and
that the young man was assuredly undrugged,
but was clearly both enjoying and loathing
what was being done to him. Another mage
of the cabal, a fat man I never cared for, came
to him and began chanting before my master
and the young man, in time to my master's
thrusts and the young man's cries.

I noticed then, that not a single one of the women of the cabal was present, and I tried to will myself back into my body, but found myself trapped within the conjury as the rite continued.

My master spoke, and it seemed he spoke right to me as he did so. "This student has broken the rules of his apprenticeship," my master said his eyes bearing into me. "He left his master's house, and lay with a woman not of our people, and he used his powers upon her to seduce her."

The fat man bowed before my master, his head beneath the altar of his apprentice's flesh. "I take full responsibility, my master," the fat man said to Master Gregory. "He is a wretched boy and shall be destroyed if it is your desire."

My master, who had withdrawn himself from the apprentice and now stood, body dripping with sweat, his gray robe spattered with fine drops of blood from the apprentice's back, turned the altar so that his face was at his waist. He made sounds of supplication to my master and begged to not be harmed, and my master thrust himself inside of the apprentice's mouth, working as hard as he had from the other direction while the apprentice coughed and gagged.

After what seemed an eternity, my master discharged himself, and I noticed now that several shadowy figures stood behind him, transparent even to the eyes of my spectral form. It was to these things my master spoke next, in a language I not only did not speak but did not even recognise.

One of the spectral beings answered, and my master laughed. He asked the apprentice what he felt he should do, and the apprentice begged to be given another chance at all costs. My master decreed that since the young man had treated an outsider as a whore, he should serve as a whore to the cabal, to right the wrong.

Through his tears, the apprentice thanked my master for the kindness of the punishment and begged him to allow him to continue to service him that night, but my master looked right into my eyes, invisible to the congregation, and decreed that his punishments this night were reserved for another and that the "boy" was to stay tied to the altar until the lusts of all the others were sated and then he would be allowed to return to his master.

He was told, without a shadow of doubt, that if he so much as looked at another woman until his apprenticeship was over, he would be forced to castrate himself, a threat the boy clearly believed.

At that, my master excused himself and walked to the door. The moment the door was opened, I found myself back in my body, still wrapped in the bandages, my eyes and ears blocked. The bandages were hot and sticky, especially between my legs, and I flushed with shame that the horrors done to the young man had so stimulated me.

I felt myself lifted off of the floor. There was a vibration, as if a zipper was pulled across me and I suddenly began spinning. There was no up or down, and I quickly began to get queasy and hyperventilate. I felt that if I could only get a touch of the floor or my torturer, who I was certain was my master, the world would resolve itself into up and down and everything would be alright.

I was ignored, then, and eventually the visions returned, but my way to the conjury was blocked, so I found myself floating around the countryside. I was later to discover that what I had encountered in the room, the visions I had seen had been what Modern Diabolists call *sensorum vitae*, which is the feminine ability to completely experience the senses of another. These can be the singular senses, as one might see, hear, feel or taste what another is experiencing, or they can be the full *sensorum*, which is every sense and feeling of another. What I had experienced was both the movement of the self out of the body (called by some astral travel but, in actuality, quite a different thing altogether) and the collective *sensorum* of the fragment of the cabal gathered for the punishment above.

My punishment for the intrusion would come later, as I experienced the *sensorum* of another punished in the same manner. By being tapped into the sensations of this other, I was able to sense that the "punishment" was not only frightening and somewhat painful but immensely pleasurable to those who found themselves punished in such a way. These punishments were for show, even (if I may be bold) for the titillation of the punishee, who always seemed charged with just enough petty crime against the cabal to get what they secretly desired, and therefore never wished to wander.

That is the secret of secrets when it comes to the groups that operate under Diabolist laws. If you give people what they secretly want but fear to ask for, you hold power over them, and if you hold power over them, you can teach them to hold power over themselves.

I was to provide further entertainment to my master and his wife that evening, but the cabal was not to be witness to it. At first I thought this a thing of shame, because I could not be compared to a human in my thoughts at that time and wanted to demonstrate to my betters that I was worth *something*. However, as I have said earlier, my master wished to make me a leader of those less than human, not less than human myself. To do this, I had to first become as they are, and this would unlock within me a desire to stay that way forever. This desire would constantly be the razor's edge I walked as a Diabolist. I would choose to rule, rather than be ruled, even as my body screamed to be ruled.

Chapter Seven: Some rules of Diabolism

I have already provided you many of the rules of Diabolism in this work, partially because it is difficult to describe Diabolism without describing the laws it works under.

The primary belief, and thus law, of Diabolism is that the underlying social system of any culture is inherently corrupt and corrupting, and that if the pressure caused by this corruption is not released the culture itself will fail. Corresponding with this belief is the feeling that the inherent social system of a culture is a necessary evil–something that *must* exist in order for society to work properly.

Another law of Diabolism that many find particularly interesting is the idea that children, as creatures without will, need to be protected from the wills of others. Society and social structures that teach that a family has a mother and father, good people succeed and bad people are punished and if you work hard you will succeed are needed for children to be raised. These social structures are much like Father Christmas, a lie we tell to make the kids happy, a way to make the harsh world less harsh. As the brain of a child develops, and the harsh world becomes something they can understand, they figure it out for the most part, and the mild upbringing they received allows them to make informed choices. They can be a part of sensible society and continue the pattern of sweetness and light for their kids and those of others or be a part of the whistle on the kettle and allow the tensions of society to blow through them.

I spoke earlier of liminality, and this is a third law within Diabolism. Mankind is an animal, with animal urges and needs, and also a God, with the capacity to create his world. Mankind is *both* animal and God, and *neither* animal *nor* God. The reason it was important that I go mad was to live life completely as an animal. This animal creature in me needs sex and affection and food and will forgo all other things to avoid discomfort. By becoming it, I could identify it.

Identifying our animal needs and separating them from ourselves is the first step towards understanding our godhood, the power of the divine that is within us. The Diabolist tradition is necessarily Promethean. We believe our divine nature, our spark, is the result of the adversary. The *Theos*, whether he be understood as Allah or YHWH, Zeus or Odin, does not want us to be creatures of will. He wants us to be obedient warriors, dying for our God. He wants us to die on the cross, to die in war, to die in the writhing pain disobedient creations deserve.

We, as Diabolists, prefer the adversary's view. He wants us to die in ecstasy, to live life to the fullest, the most absolute. We are his Bacchants, his whores and his gluttonous celebrants, feeding our animal needs because of our godly understanding of them. We revel in our limited bodies and stretch our understanding of them, indulging so as to be at one with the godhead.

We, you see, as animals, can experience the base and degrading in ways the gods cannot. When we volunteer to the whip, serve another human as if we were chattel, allow our bodies to be passed around as sacrament, perform sexual acts which could never result in procreation and otherwise debase ourselves before the divine we are not merely showing our animal nature but also flaunting it. We are gods who are animals, and even if the gods lower themselves to sexual contact with us, they can never experience the level of ecstasy we can. We burn with the flame of mortality, our lives short but brilliant, while the gods are sentenced to long low smoulders.

If the gods burned as we did they would then need to engage in petty wars as we do, so it is to our benefit that they lack our desires. This is another law of Diabolism—we perform these acts to flaunt our superiority to the gods while demonstrating our inferiority to them. We show that we are *different* from the gods, and this both pleases and angers them, which creates the energy of liminality that we, as Diabolists, feed upon.

The law of liminality is taken further by the idea of good and evil. The good (or should I say *talented*) mage is neither good nor evil. He expends immense amounts of energy on doing good and then doing evil. For every Right Hand Path mage there must be a Left Hand Path mage, so the Diabolist chooses either to serve as some Right Hander's opposite number or balances the good and the evil within his own actions. Every selfish act is countered with a selfless one, or a selfless one by proxy, and the mage completely avoids any laws of return or karma.

The most powerful good mages of our time are actually Diabolists in hiding. Some of them are as skilled with the so-called dark side as with the light and others use a known Diabolist to balance their energies when doing large workings. A good example is the many rituals to protect London from terrorist and wartime bombings. These rituals simply are not as powerful today as in the past because the bulk of the London metaphysical community does not work together to protect their home field. If Diabolists and sparkly White Witches worked together, invoking the sacred and the profane to protect that city, no terrorist would ever succeed there again— instead the Diabolists are too self-centred to ask and the fuzzy White Witches too priggish to accept even if they were asked.

That is a defacto law in Diabolism—if you can get the purest to work in your ritual you can affect a greater change than the usual metaphysical one. If you can do a rite in which your hatred is your power and your altar is one who holds no hate you can literally have no limits to your work. I was to learn this lesson when my master brought in a new female apprentice, a young White Witch of the purest goodness and most gracious of Witch lineages.

In the past two generations, the invention of Wicca as a religion has greatly reduced the number of true mage lines, or at least driven them into hiding. Magical talents, at least the very strong ones, seem to act like recessive genes. Some families in the past carefully wed and bred within other families to maintain the power of their children and it was those children who became the truly great mages—Diabolist, Pellar, White Witch, Weather Witch, Sea Hag, Ceremonial, the type did not matter, the power did. These families did not, themselves, practice a form of magic, but often trained in disparate forms of magic to bring the skills back to the family for the defence of the family.

Wicca has leeched into the environment and made it terribly unfashionable to claim magic exists in the blood and is stronger in some than others. It possesses an egalitarian, communistic view of magic it inherited from Crowley—anyone can do it, regardless of upbringing. Diabolists opposed this at first, but later were sucked into the whole notion that breeding for magical ability was somehow wrong. Shortly thereafter the major Diabolist organizations all fell into disrepair, disrepute and eventual obscurity.

Add this to the shameful fact that we have a British Diaspora with carefully bred magical families moving overseas due to financial burdens and losing touch with the land which pumps the blood in their veins and you spread the magical gene so thin that you get an entire population that can do a *little* magic instead of some few that can do a lot of magic. This is what Crowley had in mind with his creation of his metaphysical system-take the power out of the hands of the mages and place it in the hands of the people, make the Natural Nulls the rulers and the batteries and the rest rare freaks.

Siobhan, the student who my master would bring into the cabal next was a throwback to the older way of training mages. She was the daughter of one of our cabal members and a daughter of one of the metaphysical families of some repute of the south. Perhaps expectedly, she was also a distant cousin of my own, and my master relished the thought of having us both in training.

I have mentioned before that Diabolists decide upon the eventual placement of the student the moment they are added to the cabal. Siobhan was there to learn her father's ways and move on, but the hope was that she could serve as a counterpoint to my own hatred in ritual. Even though I was moving on and getting over the terrible things of my childhood, I was still a little ember of hatred, and it coloured all of my actions, and kept me from becoming a true mage and Diabolist.

Siobhan was to change that.

Chapter Eight: The Black Book

Diabolists, most famously as pirates in the seventeenth century, have a belief in fatalism and the inability of mankind to change his stars. We were born to be what we are, and the sooner we sign our names to The Black Book and swear fealty to the adversary the sooner we find the true path we were meant to take. When you hit that path, just walking it is enough to make you a stronger mage than most others. You are a star on your path through the night sky, not merely a human, and you can only be pulled from that path by a greater star than yourself.

I had signed The Black Book to serve the adversary until I was called to serve him elsewhere, but Siobhan, pale skinned and with eyes like little black pearls, had signed another book altogether. She was my age, although I felt as though she was younger, and had this delicate, vicious look about her, like a mink or a badger. She was soft, both to the touch and in her speech, but there was a feeling about her like she could tear you apart without a second thought.

While she was selfless and decidedly Right Hand Path in her views, she had this longing inside of her to test the boundaries of the path she was on. Since I was still very much a creature of my emotions, I was given to her as a subject of study and a personal servant.

Most of the time, she objected to my serving her in any but the most mundane ways. This riled my desires, of course, and left me wanting her more and more, but at the most she allowed me to wash her clothes and make her bed.

My nightmares had stopped sometime before, so when I was given over to her I felt alone but did not feel the effects of my earlier solitude. I had no sexual contact with anyone in the cabal save a perfunctory screwing at a party for the elevation of one of our younger mages to the inner circle. While I served Master Gregory at that function, he didn't even meet my eyes, and I found myself looking through the crowd for Siobhan, who merely watched with a scientific disinterest, as if my master was doing nothing more than taking care of some minor bodily function that did not warrant even a second glance.

I found myself getting furious, so once Master Gregory finished I walked through the house looking for a space that was not occupied with the merriment of others. My small cell was empty, but I could hear the vigorous fucking of a couple in the room next door, so I quickly left and found myself in the conjury, which was untidy from the ritual of elevation earlier, which I was not allowed to witness.

With nothing better to do I started cleaning the remains of the ritual up, taking the curtains down and folding them up in a basket to be laundered, removing the trash and half melted candles. I felt my consciousness slipping away until I literally became a robot, cleaning because that was part of my job. At one point Master Gregory came in, but when I stopped what I was doing he simply waved a hand to tell me to carry on and I did so. After a few hours the noises disappeared and the walls began to shine. The smell of the incense faded and the conjury began to take its day-time smell of fresh washed fabric and woodsoap.

It was as I paced the room, looking for more work in need of doing that I noticed Siobhan watching me from the doorway. I raced to kneel before her and found myself asking her, *begging* her, to give me something to do.

This caused her a great deal of distress and she turned to the shadows where Master Gregory stood and asked what to do. At that moment I felt even more worthless. I was so worthless that even an apprentice had no need for me!

I didn't understand how he answered her. Latin and Greek are as easy as English for me, but this was an ancient Brythonic tongue, and spoken specifically to exclude me. She shook her head a few times, and then said something that shocked my master into a single word of English: "Really?"

She said something affirmative, and my master ordered me to set out the candles for a ritual. It seemed odd in the diffuse glow of the morning sunlight through the frosted glass ceiling of the conjury, but I did so, even as the sky began to cloud over and the sky went from rosy morning to blue gray dusk. I was so glad for the contact from her, even as she returned to her silence and disinterested scientific stares. My master and she raised a temple within the place, their voices entwined in a harmony that seemed to literally come from paradise and hell at once. I could feel the energies of the two like two great bonfires to either side of me as they led me to the great altar, with its chains and ropes. These were not affixed to me. Instead, I was lead past the altar to the eastern wall. The curtains were parted and the walls I had cleaned with such abandon were exposed. Small but sturdy steel eyebolts stuck out of the wood, I was familiar with them from much polishing, but I had never seen them used.

Now they held some of the cuffs and chains I had cleaned so many times as part of my apprenticeship. I stepped into them, a dutiful servant, and tried to not notice how my nipples hardened at the prospect of touch and attention from the two of them. I was desperate for any meaningful touch from either, but they merely silently and tactfully attached me to the wall.

With the chains and cuffs it was rather like the sensory depravation experiences, but I could see and hear. My head was fixed into a collar and a headband of sorts which had chain fed through them and over me in such a way as to lock my head into place and my focus onto the altar. A gag was placed into my mouth and Master Gregory and Siobhan went out of sight to the sides of me. At that moment it seemed the brewing storm finally broke, and the hall literally shook with the thunder. A light flashed before my eyes, and when my vision cleared I saw not Master Gregory and Siobhan but the monster that had molested me and my own body. I watched, unable to even blink my eyes as moments I know only one person on Earth had seen were re-enacted in front of me. I watched my own self go from innocence to rage over and over again, straining against the chains to try to stop the inevitable from occurring.

We Diabolists do not lament the past, because the past makes us what we are. We punish those who harm us, but we know that nothing can stop destiny. I watched myself age at the hands of the brute, saw myself learn and improve upon the ill informed magic he tried to do. As I witnessed this again and again, I watched as the man lost power. The child saw him as a great monster, but the adult saw him for the sick weakling he was, consumed by needs he could control but chose not to. He got smaller and smaller in my esteem, until I did not look upon him with rage but with scorn. He wasn't a mage, he wasn't even a capable lover, and that innocent he killed again and again, turning it into this mewling whimpering creature allowed it to continue for years not out of fear of his actions, although that is what started it, but out of fear of being alone.

I realized that was why loneliness
brought dreams of this excuse for a man to
haunt me. I had reached a point in his abuse
where I was afraid he would stop. It wasn't
that I enjoyed or wanted it, but as long as it
was occurring I could not be surprised by
something terrible happening. Something terrible was already happening, and it was less
frightening than what the world could bring
me next.

I watched as he promoted these thoughts
in me, and saw my starry eyed self agree with
his grasping excuses, which I equated with
learning magic at the time but which were
really nothing more than his trying to keep the
authorities off of him. I watched as he saw me
grow into womanhood and how that killed
my appeal for him and how his eyes had
started to wander to other youngsters in my
area. I watched myself study the spell, fight
Master Gregory for the mandrake and still
come out victorious. In the end, I watched
him die.

The scene flipped and changed and I
watched a member of the cabal argue with
Gregory that a damaged girl could not be a
mage whatever he saw in me. I watched him
plead my case and finally summon to himself
the true Black Book, the book of fate that
holds the name of every Diabolist in it. He
found my name therein, and pushed others
aside to get me here, only to have me end up
reverting to that same mewling creature in the
end.

The chains fell away and I found myself stepping toward the altar. Gregory offered me a sword, and I saw myself, that mewling creature, and I looked him in the eye as I killed it, once and for all.

As I struck it dead it morphed into Siobhan, who was unharmed. Feelings passed through me, rage that she'd seen that, thankfulness that she worked the spell that helped me see clearly and a feeling of unworthiness. And yet, inside, I knew she was my lesser, deriving some sick enjoyment from watching my transformation into the mage that stood before her now.

It was as if a blade of cold steel had been inserted into my heart, only instead of killing me, it made me stronger. I lifted her with one hand and threw her on the altar.

"Gregory," I said, feeling no need to add an honorific to his name, "There is an intruder in the conjury."

He looked at me sideways, then smiled and nodded. "Whatever shall we do with her?" he wondered wistfully.

I bound her hands to the altar, and ripped open her white dress. "I'm certain you were not allowed in the conjury," I told her.

"But. I.," she gasped as I roughly handled her body, "I thought, I helped, I mean."

"I..I...I," I mocked. "For a Right Hand Pather, you sure talk about yourself a lot! You agreed that if you entered the conjury without permission you accepted the consequences, did you not?"

Right Hand Pathers don't like to lie, especially inside conjuries with the gods and the spirits called in as observers in a live ritual. She nodded, and prepared to be molested or worse. I lay atop her and ordered Gregory to make love to me.

We made love for hours, and I occasionally used the *sensorum* to make sure she felt just enough of my pleasure to long for it. Her father, the Diabolist, had sent her here to temper her—if she was to turn to our side, she had to do so willingly, and even though she ached for the pleasure she felt and heard me experience, my flesh pressed into hers as Gregory obeyed my demands, and I refused to let her have it unless she asked.

When I saw my name in The Black Book, I knew that hers was not there. Even as she ached for the darkness between her legs, it would be denied her forever, and since I would always know it, I knew I would have a Right Hand Pather willing to serve as my opposite number...she would always know I had the opportunity, the means and even the right to give her the darkness she lusted for and refused, and no matter what spells she and Gregory had done, she would always owe me.

Chapter Nine: Mage

Psychodrama is the easiest form of magic that Diabolists use. Using chemicals to create suggestibility, hypnosis and *sensorum vitae* to know the content of the past, mages can recreate the events of the past and change what was done. The abused can destroy their abuser, which can create such a giant vacuum in reality that the universe has no choice but to remove the person from itself to destroy the vacuum.

Siobhan had nobly sacrificed herself into my *sensorum* and faced a lesser form of the terror I had experienced. In doing so, she allowed me to realize the power of my present. I suddenly resented the animal that had bowed and scraped to Gregory. I felt as if I was an entirely different being.

There was still the matter of the apprenticeship oath. It was nearly two years since I first swore it, and I had no doubt whatsoever that I was Gregory's equal in power now that the last blockages to my power were gone. As a *Sculpere*, however, I was limited in my ability to actually generate power, and as the apprentice of the master of the cabal, I had to call him out as well as the cabal.

I told him I was ready to ascend in our cabal into the position of inner circle, and that if he was willing to call the cabal, I was genuinely prepared to call out one of the members of the inner circle. If I bested them, I would be guaranteed placement into the inner circle, and they would be required to serve me for one year to show their humiliation for losing.

Gregory assumed that I intended to call out one of the newer members, and was pleased to see his student ascend so rapidly, so he gave me a month, and told me to prepare.

I was limited in my ability to generate power, but not use it, so I spent hours in the conjury practicing just one technique, the ability to seem to be just a small distance from where I was. I knew I'd have just one chance, so I carefully prepared and at last the time came.

The cabal was assembled. Members I still did not know by name were present as I entered the room not in the white robe of an apprentice but in a street fighter's outfit of black jeans, my leather jacket and a black shirt. I stood in the centre of the conjury with my back to Gregory. I announced myself to the cabal and its host and went through the ritual questions, who was I, why was I here and, at last, Gregory's voice boomed out, "and who do you call out?"

I turned and looked him in the eyes, watching the shock cross his face as I raised my hand to point at him. "You, my master," I said with a bow.

If you are unfamiliar with the workings of a cabal, you may be surprised to find out that this shocked the circle of people in the room into angry mumbling. It is not unusual for the apprentice to call out her master, but it is unusual for an apprentice to call out her master when her master is the head of the cabal. In essence, I was calling to be elevated to the position he held, despite the fact that I was well within my rights to ascend to the inner circle by calling out another.

Gregory leapt over the altar with the same grace that got him over the churchyard wall. He had a fencer's body, and accuracy. His intention, I saw at once, was to knock me down fast and hard. I released the spell I'd worked on, and he missed me, overcompensating and nearly sending him sprawling on the floor. As he passed, I ripped the ointment of horse liniment and mandragora from within my jacket and smeared it on the back of his neck. A nearly lethal dose, delivered instantly through the skin. We shared the dose, but my tolerances were higher, as I'd been doing mandragora visions since I was a preteen.

His second lunge connected, and I was thrown back against the altar. By then the room was already starting to pulse with the hallucinogen, but I needed time. Suddenly my personal monster was standing before me, in all his reeking, towering desperation. I lost a beat to panic that was more shock than fear, then thrust the *sensorum* from my mind into his.

Women feel more than men do. This is why we get more emotional than men on occasion. Our skin is literally adapted to tell the slightest difference in firmness between two berries, our hearing and eyesight stronger and more defined. My *sensorum* of fear and abuse overwhelmed him for a moment, and it was all the space I needed to find a chink in his armour. Immediately spotting his weakness, I did another *sensorum*, this one of age and infirmity—his fear. It was less real than that built of my own experience, but it was real enough for him to stagger, and in moments I had the ritual knife poised at his throat.

First his head bowed in what I thought was shame. As he spoke the words that meant he was yielding, he looked up at me through smiling tears and a clear sense of victory. The words that pledged him to my service for a year came next, and before they were finished, two of his former subordinated had called me out.

As was permitted of the head of the cabal, I named Gregory my second and watched as he crushed their revolt with swift physical strikes, even though he was still reeling from the drugs. My bodyguards now numbered three.

Chapter Ten: Adept

The necessity to train harder and longer was thrust upon me. If I'd remained as Gregory's apprentice and took a place in the inner circle, my training as an adept would've been swift and intense but still would've taken a minimum of a year. Now I was in the position of needing to acquire the skills of an adept in a matter of months, as I could not allow my three bodyguards to protect me for the whole of my reign.

After a year I had the right to step down as I chose, but for a year I was stuck as a leader of the cabal, unless I lost the position through incompetence or weakness. I had a number of advantages over my opponents. As a woman, and a master of the *sensorum vitae*, I had a fairly good chance of weakening any male opponent with his personal fear. With Gregory as my personal servant, I could learn what he knew of each of the cabal's members, including their fears.

I built a library of remembered *sensorum*, exposing myself to the fears of each person where possible, vividly imagining it when not. That mostly took care of the cabal, but the fact remained that I was a mage in charge of adepts, and was required to be first amongst peers. I currently was not.

My previous study and the strength that came with the dissolution of my blocks was enough to rank me above most of the mages in our group. Studying magic in the past, I understood the terms and theory, but without my channels opened to the world my knowledge did not expand into the practical. Now that it was more than theory I learned fast but not fast enough to stop the rumours that our cabal was now up for conquer from any Diabolist group with enough will.

People who know nothing about magic assume a magical attack when they get a cold or a bad feeling. I tell you if you are attacked by people who know what they are doing you have no doubt what is going on. By the fifth lightning strike on the manor, people were starting to get suspicious in the town, and my first job was to put their fears at ease.

I called the members of the cabal who I could trust to help strengthen the shields of the house and convince other cabals and similar sources to look elsewhere. Even with that additional casting, I knew that I didn't have enough strength to face another cabal as a leader.

The time had come for a world walk, the practice of using mandragora or other compounds to thrust the spirit so completely into the other world that entities who reside there can be drafted into service.

My first world walk was to see the entity known in English as the Sacred Whore, a Babylonian entity that opposes the Judeo-Christian deity. We prepared a salve of travelling, and set up a temple to her, using a stone from one of her most ancient temples as a focus. It was not the first time Gregory prepared this walk, but it was my first time, so there was a lot of fear.

Whether you believe the adversaries are deities on their own or mental creations of a human shared consciousness, the fact remains that as you increase the number and type of them "in your court" you increase the power of your cabal and also the responsibilities of the cabal. In exchange for the protections we had, I ended up engaging in some form of worship or votive offering more days than not.

Since our society is more uptight about sex than anything else, forbidden sexual acts and sexual acrobatics are enough offerings for most of the adversaries. Giving yourself, or a subordinate, completely into the control of a being that some understand as having been created fully from mankind's lust is often a good start, and while many have experienced the touch of the adversary when engaging in these acts without the aid of ritual or psychoactive compounds, these later things heighten the experience.

One of the problems with this, of course, is that it gets incredibly difficult to find satisfaction in any other way. The adversary takes over so completely that simple sexual needs are subsumed into this desire to enter into the secret place of sin and shame again and again, as if your suffering and pleasure can somehow ease the suffering of the world and fill it with pleasure.

There are places in the east where nascent Christianity, generally less than three hundred years old, results in otherwise sane native men literally nailing themselves to crosses on Good Friday, believing the spasms of pain and suffering bring them closer to their God, and remove sin from the world. Our less dramatic journeys of suffering and pain have a similar result. We remove the sins of the world by taking them upon ourselves.

The Sacred Whore taught me the technique of reflection. I could look into a man or a woman and be exactly what he or she wanted. I could be weak or strong, aggressive or a victim, and always be in control the entire time. This reflection was particularly handy when enacting the role of Sacred Whore myself.

From The Satyr I learned the technique of abandon. I could either completely lose control of my own body or cause others to lose their own control. This was the ultimate in catharsis. Literally the human within the animal shell dies and the animal shell is all that remains. You become a machine wishing only to breed, eat, drink and breed some more. When you emerge from it, you are reborn as more human than you were before.

From The Murderer I learned the power of loss and rage, the ability to turn off emotion and become the literal Hand of God. I reached into the heart and mind of a suicide killer, and faced the conviction of being completely right, with no doubt of my actions. I learned to turn this from rage and obedience into the cold hard steel of will.

The Betrayer, The Fury, The Wretch, The Accuser, The Prince of Lies. Each of them was an aspect and a talent, and I paid the price for each to learn how to do things I only understood in theory before. I grew from theory to practice in a matter of weeks, and by the second meeting, I oozed the appropriate level of power to silence even my most voracious critics.

The *sensorum* was the most important technique in my arsenal, however. Most people, even outside the Diabolist community, have experienced some form of the *sensorum*, generally when a particularly empathic musician has imparted emotion into a song. This emotion will transcend recording media, but when you actually are present you can close your eyes and see the images in the musician's mind, feel the emotions and even the sensation of the instrument or microphone in the mage's hand. The *sensorum* is a technique that builds upon this.

Women are nearly always superior in projecting the *sensorum* because we experience life with a higher degree of sensitivity. Our fingers, lips and skin detect pressure, heat and vibration at a higher level and lower baseline than the male of our species. Men are better at directive magic—moving force from one place to another. Women, on the other hand, are the masters of sensation.

If you find this hard to believe, a journey into the "unmentionables" department of any major chain store should put it to rest. While an equal number of silk and fine fabrics will be found in the men's section, you will feel threads on the seams, elastic bands and plastic buttons that rest on the skin that will never be in the majority of female undergarments. Women would never put up with the sensations of these things against their skin, not because we are the weaker sex but because we are literally more sensitive. We feel grains in fabric, seams and folds and other things that men will never detect.

That is not to say that no men are born with the level of sensitivity a woman has. On the contrary, some men can feel just as much as women do, but they are essentially feminine in their mystical energies. They may express themselves as homosexual, but this is not necessarily the case, and certainly there are straight male mages with a high degree of *sensorum.*

The talent of *sensorum* is generally mixed with a high degree of sensitivity to the world, so the strongest natural projectors of *sensorum vitae* tend to be allergic to things, overly emotional and the very first person to detect a gas leak, spilled perfume or other irritants. These people are nearly disabled by their perception of reality, but as a result can call upon the memories of a sensation so completely that they can overwhelm the sensory input of the person they are projecting into.

When men do the *sensorum*, it tends to be unisensorial, that is to say it will be an extreme physical sensation, taste, sound or vision. This is generally called sense illusion or sense hijacking, and is easiest to do when a person is missing sensory data–suspended in an isolation tank or black room, or hanging in a sensory deprivation bag. If the person is in a suggestible state (or weak-willed) it is even easier.

Just as many men can learn to use the *sensorum* nearly as clearly as women do with practice, so too can women learn to hijack just one sense at the same time. Imagine the power, for example, of the taste sensation of vomit projected upon an enemy as he ate dinner or the sensation of knives while he makes love to his woman. The cold, silk touch of a snake crawling up the arm of a man terrified of snakes, a sensation he will do anything to avoid, can drive a man to suicide or self mutilation properly applied.

Most practice in *sensorum* begins in the bedroom, one sense at a time. First you focus upon fully feeling the sense, and then you push it upon your partner. It is difficult to describe the push. If you visualize the sensation as a light, you can imagine your partner absorbing the light, but this isn't a really accurate description. Usually trial and error is enough to get you to the early stages, and once you've figured out the basic sensation of pushing sensory input or a sense memory into someone it all falls into line. The ultimate test, of course, is pressing a sense that you never experienced personally into a person who is actively fighting you. Doing it from a distance is particularly difficult, but it is all variation on the first sensation.

When I was a child, my mother (who was a New Ager, not really a mage) would practice this with me by sitting across the table from me with a screen between us and having cups of hot and cold water. As she dipped fingers in each one, I learned to reach out and know which hand (left or right) and whether the water was hot or cold. By the age of ten I could tell her not only hot or cold and the hand, but which finger on the hand it was. I imagine this would be a good experiment for a beginner to try, but no beginner should experiment with Diabolism.

The Right Hand Path is the nursery of Diabolism. It is a safe place to practice your skills and learn new ones without worrying about the law of cause and effect. Since their focus is on healing the world and fighting evil, the skills you learn on The Right Hand Path are invaluable once you are ready to enter Diabolism. New Diabolists with little power who can find a teacher willing to teach them are often eaten alive[7] by Diabolists—their powers and abilities burned away in singular rituals their masters are unwilling to face the aftersickness for doing themselves.

That's not to say all Right Hand Pathers become Left Hand Pathers, just that the dark

---

[7] Not *literally!*

little sparks of tortured gothic souls that want to be Darth Vader when they grow up inevitably get used up and tossed out by Diabolists, so the smart ones find themselves Masters who aren't going to use them up, and most of them tend to be Right Hand Pathers or the rarer Gray or "Centre" mages.

My New Age mother, my interest in magic as a child, even the abuse I'd survived, all added up to help me be better prepared to be a strong mage when the time came. Anything that increases your knowledge of your will and your innate abilities can be turned to your advantage, no matter how terrible. That's not to say terrible things are preferred—because those things must be dealt with and finished before your training in magic can be complete. As the saying goes, what doesn't kill us makes us stronger.

The move from mage to adept for me was extraordinary. I went from being a mage with an uncommon amount of technical knowledge to an adept with an uncommonly small amount of practical experience in a matter of months. If anyone tells you book smarts aren't helpful in metaphysics—laugh at them.

As an adept, I could remove myself from the physical and fully sense the energy flows in the universe. This allowed me to more efficiently tap the land for power, which reduced the aftersickness of a major working. It is only the simplest of mages who will leave themselves open to tremendous aftersickness in any planned working. Called out by a major mage into a personal duel and making yourself sick is acceptable, but given time and planning if you make yourself ill all you do is prove your ineptitude.

I also had the benefit of an unbreakable bond between myself and Siobhan, which meant that whenever her little group released energy into the universe to "heal it," I could tap into that and use it to fill back in the spaces of magic I drained from the area. It is difficult to turn energy that is directed by a trained will to a purpose contrary to that mage's direction, but with subtlety, one can interpret the meaning of a vague direction to one's own purpose.

Chapter Eleven: Defending the Conjury

Most of my energies were now directed into building more energy reserves for the cabal and the conjury. I had started as an apprentice by strengthening the shields with my energy, and now as an adept I had to add to them. Visualisation is a chief component in magic. You form the desire within your mind and then use the magic to make that desire reality. Any magical or metaphysical system that does not teach visualisation first and foremost is a joke, as even the least experienced mage skilled in visualisation is superior to an experienced mage who cannot visualise.

Visualisation is a poor term, since a good visualisation uses all seven of the mage's senses—touch, taste, hearing, vision, smell, detection of energy and place in space/time. Most of us are familiar with the first five of these, but the last two are equally important. Energy detection is the core sense in magic. It consists of knowing how much energy you have, the energy sources around and within you and the ability, even if unskilled, to move these sources to your benefit.

If you are training your ability to hear as part of your visualisations, you might try to remember every detail of a song until you hear it playing in your head. With the energy detection sense, you use your mind to move the energy to increase your skill with it.

Place in space/time is a well researched, if poorly understood sense. An exceptional example of this is found in most gymnasts, who can flip and turn and roll on a mat and still know exactly where up and down and right and left are, even as the fluids in their inner ear are cast into complete disarray. A strong sense of place in space and time can remove you from the drug induced haze of a working, or allow you to step out of the current world and into a new one by will alone.

Visualisation allows you to create a world in the mind and force the outer world to come into alignment with it by force of will. Both the power required to force the universe to comply with your will and the ability to masterfully create visualisations are difficult to explain in plain language. It's sort of like describing a colour to a blind person, in that if you've never experienced it, you lack the vocabulary to understand it and you if have experienced it, you know no words will suffice.

Although Gregory accepted me as leader and I'd managed to win the cabal to my side, there was still the problem of the other cabals, and their view of me as an impetuous upstart who'd taken the highest group in with simple tricks and cleverness.

Cabals are necessarily territorial. Too many Diabolists in an area and the common folk start picking up on the fact that things are going on. Already our town was suspect, a local "medium," whose only power was the ability to observe things very well had decided that the comings and goings of the local unchurched men and women of power to

Gregory's house meant something was going on. She wrote in her local paranormal newspaper about ley lines on our street, Witches and Faeries and worse, which let to an influx of new faces peering in.

A few words to Siobhan and her family allowed us to plant the rumour that we were mere Witches, likely of the Gardnerian stripe, and that we valued privacy, and the tattler's people stopped coming around, many of them Witches of one stripe or another. The warning chilled us though, if someone like this snoop had picked up that we were not engaged in regular life, then it was likely people who the common folk would believe would start to pick it up.

That meant taking care of the two cabals from neighbouring areas who had stepped up their activities in what they perceived as a territorial opening. The first trick was to try parley. Of the two groups, only one agreed to meet in person, and then only after I'd sent a member of our cabal right to their door, making it clear we knew where they were.

When Gregory had started his cabal, the Diabolist movement was largely dead outside the major cities. He had started with just his wife, his brother and a school friend, under the tutelage of an elderly man who'd been part of Diabolism at its height and remained true to his beliefs following the nadir of Diabolism during the Second World War. Diabolism suffered terribly at that time, with our main leaders dead or dying, our bright young things away at the front and our necessarily suspicious actions raising fears of spies in our neighbours. After the war, the networks of Diabolism were gone or non-functional and the rise of so-called White Witchcraft as an alternative had stripped us of many new prospects. Since those early Witches did not have the goodness and light aspects of today's Witches, many would-be Diabolists joined up, lending our superior knowledge of ceremonial magic and the way energy works to the infant that was Wicca.

When the closeted Diabolists finally got fed up and left Wicca for good in the midseventies, seeing it as irreconcilably friendly with the very churches that first caused them to rebel, they found the vast networks they'd experienced as children gone. Gregory, related by blood to this great Diabolist who he'd learned from, started things nearly from scratch, his only books the works of Crowley and Waite, his lifeline to the past his own very aged master.

He had a house used to rites, and his parents, although not Diabolists themselves, were eccentric enough to have many friends sympathetic to Diabolism pass through as he grew up, and one of their many borders was an American student who brought American-style Satanism to Gregory, who learned from it, then moved on.

Diabolism differs from Satanism in three major ways. Primarily American Satanism is about recognising humankind's place in the

animal kingdom and disposing of the pleas-
antries that grease the wheel of society. It is
rough, realistic and for the most part sees the
Adversary as opposed to the Judeo-Christian
God, which is why it is termed Satanism, even
though they feel Satan is a metaphor.

Diabolists feel Satan is real, a creation of
mankind's own making. When a person does
well at sport or science and thanks their God,
they give power to Satan, by saying that God
supported them and not the millions who do
not succeed. These people help divide man
into those lucky few who are men of God and
leave the common man to Satan. Satan is
given power by mankind's ignorance of God.
If God is good, and pays attention to the
world, then every bad thing that happens
must be the fault of Satan.

It does not matter that a God is neutral
at best, because the will of millions of humans
on this earth is that their God is all-powerful
and good, which means that bad that happens
must happen because of an all-powerful evil,
or a nearly all-powerful evil, and just as man
wills this all-powerful good God into being by
making his inner world reflected upon the
outer one, he wills the ultimate (or penulti-
mate) evil into existence.

Satanism is patently atheistic, there are
no gods, save those made by mankind. Diabolism believes that gods do exist, but that the
energy of the world is not determined by
gods, but by the collective will of mankind.
We take the will of evil towards mankind and

turn it into our own power, harnessing it and taking it away from those who would do the broad culture harm. On the macroscopic level, Diabolism is inherently good. We take the energy that might be levelled into the collective will of a people to create a terrorist incident against another people and use that will for personal gain. It is only at the individual level that we can be thought of as evil.

Lastly, all Satanists are generally equals, but Diabolists have levels. We have the outermost level, the disenfranchised young men and women that would fall easiest into religious indoctrination, who we easily use to fuel our powers, and we have those who know the inner mechanics of the universe and exploit them.

Without blowing our powers out of proportion, I want to make it clear that most Diabolists believe that the decline of Diabolism and the rise of religious terrorism are directly related. Religious extremists use fear and disenfranchisement to convince the disenfranchised that they have nowhere to go but to heaven, no life worth living but the afterlife, and no value as living creatures.

Get one of these young men into a Diabolist cabal; show him the pleasure of a woman, the ecstasy of the touch of the adversary, and then show him that his name is in The Black Book itself, and his life becomes worthy of preserving. We know, as Diabolists, that when we reach the innermost circle of circles, we are assured an afterlife of power and prestige, but fail as beginners, or turn from Diabolism to another faith and the true meaning of The Black Book comes to mind. You are not just the possession of the adversary, but the possession of your cabal. You do not leave Diabolism, you are here forever.

Young people, turned from their faith by pleasure, educated in the finest schools, fed and clothed and eventually wealthy by virtue of the schooling we have seen them through, never return to their previous religion. How could they? We hold their soul, inscribed of their own free will in the book of the damned, we hold them in debts of honour and money and if they go to those religious groups that sponsor terrorism, they know the undeniable truth that seeing the West, or Jews, or Christians or Atheists as Satan does not really harm those so labelled, and certainly empowers Satan.

The iron hand within the velvet glove of Diabolism is the knowledge that you may leave, but your soul will never leave, and any deity you turn to for salvation from the adversary will only strengthen the adversary and darken your name in The Black Book. Join us of your own accord and you are ours forever.

Gregory found that out as a young man, when he turned away from his teacher and towards radical Christianity. He says that while he sat there, trying to purify himself of the adversary the power grew and grew over him until every time he closed his eyes to sleep he felt himself made love to by his mas-

ter, and making love to his master as well. After three weeks of these dreams, his will broke
and he begged his master to take him back.
His master made him suffer another month
before filling his needs and showing him the
way back home.

Still, one master, a few books and
knowledge of history does not make a cabal.
Slowly, just as his master had found Gregory's
weakness, he found people who would blos-
som in the cabal: the insatiable woman who
wanted to experience sex in all its forms, the
brother with needs impossible to detail in this
book for fear of legal ramifications, the school
friend who had needed to cheat to pass a major exam. As Gregory met the needs of his
followers, he found his own needs met, and
he let the needs become rituals, the rituals become magic, and the magic become
impossible to live without.

By the time I met with them, they'd spun
off at least seven groups, and likely more, and
when I wrested control it was the first two
groups that Gregory spawned that decided to
fight us. The first, unsure of itself or its powers, met us to parley at a neutral site, a set of
standing stones off of the tourist circuit. Raising power in a duel here would likely anger
the local Witches and Neo-Druids, and we
were as much their shared enemy as Christians.

We met at midnight, hiking up the boggy
trails to the stones from appointed trails, ours
to the south off of a well travelled road, his

through a neighbouring schoolyard. Both trails meant that parking cars or otherwise leaving reinforcements would engage the suspicions of the authorities and as the man I was meeting and I would both be armed, this was a bad idea.

I travelled my appointed trail at the appointed time, a handgun Gregory had acquired in a professional capacity in a holster beneath my black leather jacket, which was now cleaned and scuffed to a deep texture almost like suede. It reflected none of the light from the passing cars as I got out and headed up.

Mine was the more difficult climb. It meandered, often descending into mushy swamp, other times a dusty and dank scramble up what was probably a waterfall in spring. As I raised higher the climb became easier, the path cut like that of a Tor, going up towards the now visible stones in a zigzag that came out at the northernmost gap within them. My adversary was waiting, similarly clothed. His boots were muddy from a similarly dank trail, although his face, reflected in the wan moonlight, showed none of the signs of climbing I was sure mine did.

I approached him, hands out, showing that I did not have a weapon in my hand and he launched like a cat, a black-bladed army knife in his hand. Gregory had prepared me for that, as it was this man's one good fighting move, and as he'd taught me I used a foot sweep and a simple kick to bring him down,

landing flat on his back. I stomped on the
wrist that held the knife and it skittered into
the darkness of the forest around us. Another
knife came out of his jacket, and I pointed the
gun at his head as Gregory had told me and
released the safety with an ominous click.

The man gulped and dropped the second
knife, putting his hands on his head like a
character in a cop drama. I stepped back, re-
engaged the safety and holstered the gun,
resuming my hands out position as he raised
himself from the ground. "I hope that is the
end of the formalities," I told him.

If I'd drawn the gun the moment I'd
reached him, it would've meant the death of
one of us, but since I'd showed the physical
prowess to fight him off coupled with the
unwillingness to expend more than a modi-
cum of energy to do so via the gun, he held a
grudging admiration for me. Diabolists, as a
rule, don't carry guns, but I was easily half the
weight of the men of the cabals in my area
and I was damned if I was going to put up
with being manhandled when I knew my way
around firearms.

There was a small outdoor table on a
cement slab near the edge of the clearing the
stones sat in, some old attempt at turning the
area to a park, and we walked to it, sitting on
the rusted steel benches across from each
other. Once there, we talked until the sun began to rise, making deals, making concessions.
I gave up three men on his side of town, he
returned four of mine who'd split when I took

control. He agreed to support me as the leader of the highest cabal of the area in return for a chance to sit beside me and upon my word that I would not fight Gregory if he intended to wrest control back. He even agreed, although it was not in his best interest, to parley with the cabal that would not meet me and make them come to an accord with him, and by extension, me.

My main job was to convince him that nothing changed, that Gregory was still the leader in my eyes and that it was formality, not will, that dictated I take his place. It is often easier to convince people of the truth than of a falsehood, and this was true enough to count. By the end of the meeting, as I began the long hike back to the road and called in my ride, I was convinced it was all going to turn out for the best, despite the odds.

When we returned to the conjury, however, it was quickly apparent things were not to be so easy. The house was covered in graffiti, spray painted pentagrams and 666es designed to call attention to the people within. The assumption, of course, would be that we were not involved with the occult, but we had angered people involved with the occult, and the hope of our attackers was that the authorities would deem the house suspicious and make trouble for us even if they thought we were innocent.

Inexplicably, Gregory had mineral spirits and paint on hand and we set to work before the paint had fully set. By the time the authorities came by, informed by an anonymous concerned individual, there was no sign of graffiti to be found, just gleaming clean stone and a newly painted door. Gregory insisted to them that their concerned individual was a neighbourhood tattler, a senior citizen who probably thought their early morning cleaning was nefarious, even though it was only carried out so early to allow them to attend a local charity dinner that afternoon.

To make sure the pretence stuck, we had to get to that very dinner, even though we were all ready to drop from exhaustion. That night, we were too tired to celebrate and just slept where we landed—on beds, sofas and even the kitchen floor.

Chapter Twelve: Peace

The addition of the Southern Cabal to our growing membership left one enemy cabal, and my words, Gregory's words and the words of our new found friend could not sway them to our side. It was they that had vandalized the house, and a number of similar incidents, both physical and metaphysical, were to follow. The only answer was overt war, and it began the very next morning.

In order for Diabolism to work, it has to stay underneath the radar of the establishment, which is why the serious Diabolists rarely look the part. Little old ladies and gentlemen, respectable members of government and church hierarchies and boring old schoolteachers are far more likely to be established Diabolists than the neo-punk with the ring in his nose and the pentagram tattoos. We must hide in plain sight for our plans to work.

The leader of our new enemy cabal got into Diabolism because of his sexual urges for both sexes, and his predilection for degrading and humiliating his partners. Like many such unsuccessful sadists, he found the most extraordinary pleasure in making his partners feel like whores, but disliked it intensely if they enjoyed his games. It was this desire for victims, as opposed to equal partners, that led to his initial split from Gregory's cabal, and this desire that we would exploit to further his destruction.

We knew of a successful and willing Lady of the Evening who had a grudge against this man, whom I'll call Colin, and was more than willing to participate in his downfall. She was well established with the authorities for her alleged crimes, the so-called oldest profession, which is one of the ways other than Diabolism that the sexual pressure gauge of culture can be released. Colin did not actually know her, but had an incident with one of the women's friends, and we offered her a substantial sum of money to assist us, even though she was prepared to do so for free.

To cut to the chase, we paid her to be caught servicing and to be temporarily incarcerated for it. She agreed with the authorities to participate in a quasi-legal set-up and we arranged for said authorities to be delayed in busting in. As a result, the actual set-up was kept from the bulk of the public, lest the authorities be called out for the questionable nature of the set-up, and the audio recording of this man being "serviced," including several expletives and names of the adversary coming out of his mouth did not make it into a court, but into the cabal's hands. Playing it only once for his mistress was enough to cost him that, and the threat of playing it for his wife and members of his parish made him decide that we were not to be fooled with any longer.

This led to a period of peace that would last until the end of my reign and the beginning of Gregory's new reign, a transition that would occur with a simple surrender and not a whisper of complaint from the masses. Peace would reign until I destroyed it in another way, but that is another story, which deserves telling at another time.

I would be lying if I said everything in here was true. There are more deceptions herein than even those of my own cabal could pick out. There is truth told as lie, and lie told as truth, in the honour of the Prince of Lies himself. Those whose names are in The Black Book and those who have faced The Black Book and not found their names therein will have no difficulty discerning truth from fiction.

There are some points I'd like to clarify as undeniably true. Diabolism is a very real thing, it does lie beneath the surface of restrictive cultures and it is assuredly strengthened when the followers of so-called good gods give power to the *adversaries* of those gods. It is practiced by adults with adults, and children of Diabolists are as protected from contact with it as any other children. We believe in the manipulation of energy and will, and without the formation of a fully trained will, you cannot be a Diabolist.

The man who abused me was a pretentious ass, one of a type of child abuser who blames his religion on his actions, no more indicative of a Diabolist than a Catholic priest buggering altar boys is indicative of a Catholic. That being said, Diabolists and pretenders to Diabolism who bring down the law upon us (as child abusers inevitably do) are gotten rid of swiftly in our ranks. If they cannot be

placed somewhere where their interaction
with youngsters is minimized, then more spe-
cific, more dramatic, actions are called for.

With the exception of the prohibitions
against using those with an unformed will and
the fact that we exist, I make no claims of va-
lidity to anything herein. Those who know
Diabolism can separate truth from fiction, and
those in places where Diabolism has died can
use the laws and examples herein to rebuild it,
or build it from scratch in the few places
where we have never reached.

In a world of religious fundamentalism,
the self-righteous give power to The Adversary in all its forms every time they lay what is
not its fault upon its feet. Their belief fuels
our rites and rituals, and we can either use that
power or ignore it. If *you* don't use it, be assured that *we* will. Love demands that we
preserve our way of life at all costs, and we
will not let the power of The Adversary that
the fundamentalists add to daily go to waste.
Love is the law.